DATE DUE

OC 8'90			
NO 23'90			
JA 26'91			
AP 17'91			
AB 21 95			
AP 20'00			
MY 06'00			
AG 24'12			

DEMCO

DISCOVER
The Shores of the Great Lakes

BY CATHERINE CALHOUN

PHOTOGRAPHY BY
JOE VIESTI

GALLERY BOOKS
An Imprint of W.H. Smith
112 Madison Avenue
New York, New York 10016

A FRIEDMAN GROUP BOOK

Published by GALLERY BOOKS
An Imprint of W. H. Smith Publishers, Inc.
112 Madison Avenue
New York, New York 10016

ISBN 0-8317-3940-1

Discover the Shores of the Great Lakes
was prepared and produced by
Michael Friedman Publishing Group, Inc.
15 West 26th Street
New York, New York 10010

Editor: James K. Blum
Art Director: Robert W. Kosturko
Photo Editor: Christopher C. Bain
Production Manager: Karen L. Greenberg

All photographs © Viesti Associates.
Viesti Associates is a stock-photography library
with offices in New York City and Austin, Texas.

Color separations by Hong Kong Scanner Craft Company Ltd.
Printed and bound in Hong Kong by Leefung-Asco Printers, Ltd.

CONTENTS

Introduction
PAGE 8

PART ONE
Lake Ontario
PAGE 10

PART TWO
Lake Erie
PAGE 20

PART THREE
Lake Huron
PAGE 32

PART FOUR
Lake Michigan
PAGE 44

PART FIVE
Lake Superior
PAGE 60

Introduction

Ever since they were discovered in 1615, the Great Lakes have challenged man's descriptive powers. Early explorers felt the word "lake" was a terrible understatement, given the magnitude of the waters. An official title change that would promote the lakes to "freshwater seas" was suggested. While that label may be technically correct, it doesn't fully express the character of these inland waters. As the region's residents know, the term "great" refers to more than the lakes' size. It also points to the beauty of their shores, the vitality of their cities, the richness of their history, and the spirit of their people.

No geographical area has served North America better than the Great Lakes. Stretching from the cosmopolitan East deep into Canada's forests and the northern plains of the United States, the Great Lakes Waterway was once the continent's lifeline. Processions of cargo ships hauled raw materials eastward, while passenger ships returned with multitudes of hopeful immigrants and hardy pioneers, feeding the region's rapid expansion.

In the late nineteenth and early twentieth centuries, the growing industrialization of the

Great Lakes area and the rise of American commerce were tightly intertwined. The lakes released the United States' vast resources. As timber, grain, copper, iron ore, and coal filled eastbound freighters, American industry no longer depended on the East Coast for raw materials. Mills, mines, and factories sprang up on the lakes' southern shores. The area's burgeoning steel industry was evident everywhere, from the Chicago-School-of-Architecture-influenced skyscrapers to Detroit's automobile empires. Adjacent dairy- and farmlands prospered, and shoreline summer enclaves sprang up as urban centers continued to swell.

This growth continued apace throughout the Second World War, until it ultimately threatened the lakes' livelihood: As recently as twenty years ago, concerned environmentalists were predicting an untimely death for the great waters. They cited increasing industrial abuse of the lakes, including widespread pollution and over-fishing. Since then, the American and Canadian governments have introduced new regulations and stringent water-quality standards, and their efforts have paid off. The lakes' troubled spots, particularly Lake Erie, have undergone miraculous transformations.

PART ONE

Lake Ontario

*O*nce a quiet, conservative city, Toronto (previous page) has become one of North America's most vibrant metropolitan areas. Its dynamic character is embodied in the Canadian National Tower. At 1,815 feet, it is the world's tallest freestanding structure. One of Toronto's most popular attractions is the multifaceted Ontario Place (previous page inset). This ninety-six acre complex sits on three man-made islands and offers a variety of cultural and recreational activities.

Over the years, Lake Ontario has acquired an unfair reputation as "the forgotten Great Lake." But any sailor who has navigated the breathtaking entrance from the St. Lawrence River could hardly forget this body of water. Westward travelers are greeted by the Thousand Islands, which crowd the lake's eastern edge before giving way to open water.

Over five million American and Canadian citizens reside on the lake's 630-mile shore. Most of them are concentrated in Canada's "Golden Horseshoe," a modern megalopolis that stretches out from either side of Toronto along the lake's western shoreline. Toronto itself has become a vigorous city in the past thirty years: When the St. Lawrence Seaway first allowed ocean-going freighters access to the lake in 1959, Canada's industrial center effectively moved inland from Montreal to Toronto, the capital of Ontario. The resulting employment opportunities attracted waves of immigrants, including large populations of Italians, Chinese, and Portuguese, as well as Germans, Hungarians, and Indians.

*T*oronto is a lively mix of old and new. After the Second World War, a wave
of immigrants moved into the city, bringing with them such traditional pastimes
as the Italian game of bocce.

*M*ore than eighteen hundred wooded islands dot the eastern end of Lake Ontario. Known as Thousand Islands, New York, they extend fifty-two miles into the St. Lawrence River.

The new residents gave the city a diverse cultural character and helped Toronto grow into a thriving, modern metropolis.

Thirty miles across the water, Lake Ontario's American shore is lined with campgrounds and picturesque vacation communities. A few miles south of the waterfront, the land is dotted with ripe orchards and vineyards. The region's unique soil mixture yields harvests of tomatoes, cherries, grapes, peaches, melons, and half of New York State's apples.

Despite the obvious enticements of cosmopolitan Toronto and the lush American farmlands, the lake's most popular tourist site is Niagara Falls. Here, the mighty Niagara River plummets 193 feet in a magnificent cascade of thundering water, mist, and spray. A breathtaking demonstration of nature's force, this natural wonder drives the world's largest hydroelectric development, which supplies the area with most of its power. The scene is romantic, too, as legions of honeymooning couples will attest. Niagara Falls' first newlywed visitors, relatives of Napoleon Bonaparte, came for a look in 1803. Soon after, a honeymoon at the Falls was *de rigueur* for wealthy couples. The attraction is still going strong.

*T*oronto's Ontario Place (below) hosts thousands of visitors each day during its May-to-September high season. Its facilities include an outdoor amphitheater, marinas, museums, pavilions, and the Cinesphere, a curved movie screen that stands six stories high and eighty feet wide.

*B*ased in Toronto, the Canadian National Exhibition (left) features parades, art exhibits, and dozens of sporting events, as well as water and air shows. The celebration has taken place during the last week in August and the first week in September for 110 years.

*I*n the early 1900s, many of the Thousand Islands (left) served as summer residences for American millionaires, whose opulent "vacation cottages" were legendary for their extravagance. Casa Loma, North America's largest castle (above), was built by a wealthy industrialist to satisfy his obsession with medieval design. The ninety-eight room palace houses dozens of moveable walls, hidden panels, and secret stairways.

PART TWO

Lake Erie

*T*he Port Stanley lighthouse presides over Lake Erie's Canadian shore. The

triangular structure is a beacon for the region's commercial fishermen and sailors.

In the early 1970s, Lake Erie became a rallying point for concerned environmentalists. At the time, the lake was suffocating from an overabundance of phosphorus and algae brought on by unchecked pollution. Erie was buffeted by bad publicity, from jokes on *The Tonight Show* to alarmist newspaper headlines that called it the second Dead Sea.

Fortunately, notices of Erie's death were premature. In the last two decades an unprecedented cleanup has brought miraculous new life to this Great Lake. Once synonymous with runaway pollution, it is now a clear symbol of public initiative and international cooperation. Today, nearly all of Erie's beaches are open for swimming, its cities are flourishing, and its commercial fishing industry has never been better, with a harvest of more than fifty million pounds annually.

Sport fishing on Erie is also a burgeoning business. The lake is recognized as "the walleye capital of the world," and when anglers catch their limit of walleye (or pickerel, as they are called in Canada), they can

Magee Marsh (previous page) in Ohio is the remnant of a three hundred thousand-acre swamp that once stretched along the southern edge of Lake Erie. The Marsh's Black Swamp Woods retain a mysterious, prehistoric quality. Lush South Bass Island (previous page inset) lies near Put-in-Bay, Ohio. Just south of this site, Commander Oliver Hazard Perry's fleet defeated the British squadron in the historic Battle of Lake Erie during the War of 1812.

*C*arrying 475 passengers per trip, the popular excursion boat Goodtime II (below) cruises Cleveland's waterfront, as did the original Goodtime almost a century ago.

*P*leasure boats and condominiums line the harbor o Catawba Island (above), near Port Clinton, Ohio. Increasing recreational activity, such as that on Catawba Island, attests t the revitalization of Erie's waterfront.

cast their lines for perch or bass. Since 1980, charterboat bookings on Erie have added more than ten million dollars to Ohio's tourist industry each year, leading Ohio's governor to call Lake Erie "the State's most valuable resource." This reacquired distinction has spurred a flurry of large-scale development along the lake's southern shore. The cities of Toledo, Cleveland, and Buffalo, once ridiculed as vehemently as the lake itself, are rebuilding their waterfronts. Projects like Toledo's Portside River Development boast shopping malls, boutiques, and lively seafood restaurants. Excursion boats cruise Cleveland's gentrified harbor area, and lucky passengers can hear an occasional waterfront concert by the Cleveland Orchestra, or simply watch the activity on the bustling banks of the cleaned-up Cuyahoga River (which was once so polluted that it actually caught fire). To further encourage recreational activity, Cleveland has planned an ambitious "inner harbor." Scheduled for completion in 1990, the seven-acre development will feature an aquarium, a maritime center, and a grand festival market.

*G*reat blue and black-crowned herons nest by the thousands on Erie's West Sister Island. Most of the birds, like this one, fly daily to Ohio's Crane Creek State Park to feed.

*T*he rocky Marblehead Peninsula in Sandusky Bay is one of the most treacherous areas for Lake Erie's mariners. Its classic lighthouse, in service since 1821, boasts the longest tenure of any watch in the Great Lakes.

*T*he sandy tip of Point Pelee National Park dips south into Lake Erie from Leamington, Ontario. Starting early each morning, regular ferry service carries passengers to nearby Pelee Island. Once struggling with widespread pollution, Cleveland—like Lake Erie—has literally cleaned up its act (following page). The city's rejuvenated waterfront will feature a multimillion dollar "inner harbor" by 1990.

PART THREE

Lake Huron

Sault Ste. Marie, Michigan's famous Soo Locks (previous page), where Lake Superior empties into St. Mary's River and Lake Huron, were a historic addition to the Great Lakes Waterway. The canals were completed in 1855, with four locks on the American side and one in Canada. What would a waterfront be without seagulls? They fly over all five of the Great Lakes (previous page inset).

One nineteenth-century diarist described the Great Lakes' residents as having "a spirit of adventurous enterprise, a willingness to go through any hardship to accomplish an object, and an independence of thought and action." This was certainly true of those who settled the shores of Lake Huron. The area's earliest inhabitants were hardy fur-traders, traveling through the waters in birchbark canoes. They built thriving tradeposts on Huron's forested Manitoulin and Mackinac islands. Those encampments later served as fueling stations for the wood-burning steamboats that brought several generations of pioneers to the territory.

With great foresight, several generations of residents near Lake Huron have made an effort to preserve the charm of their early nineteenth-century villages and the wilderness of the surrounding forests. Today, enchanting Mackinac Island is reminiscent of nineteenth-century Michigan. Its quiet hills are traveled primarily by horse-drawn carriages and bicycles, and winter snowplows are the only motor vehicles allowed on

*T*he lighthouse in Michigan's Presque Harbor was a state-of-the-art structure in 1840, when it was first lit. Now a museum, it features exhibits of antique navigational instruments.

Michigan's Mackinac Island (right) is a throwback to the nineteenth century. A resort area since the 1830s, the island's only modes of transportation are horse-drawn carriages and bicycles.

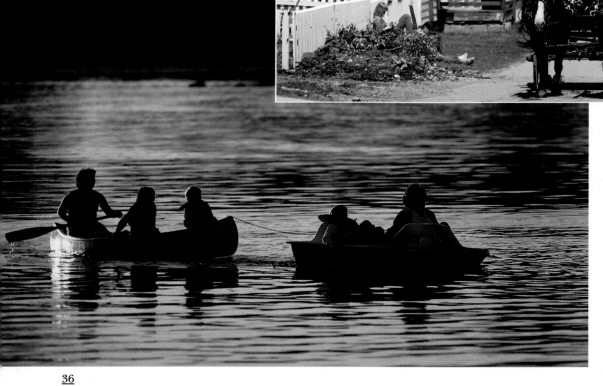

Georgian Bay (left), on the Canadian side of Lake Huron, is broken up by densely wooded islands. The area attracts visitors from both Canada and America for camping, boating, and hiking amidst its wild beauty.

the island. Not surprisingly, many visitors return to the peaceful old-worldiness of Mackinac Island year after year.

Travelers to Huron's Canadian side claim a similar devotion to its charms. Northeastern Georgian Bay, which roughly mimics Huron's form, attracts thousands of serious fishermen from Toronto, Ottawa, and Detroit. Coho and chinook salmon abound in the bay, and there are smaller numbers of whitefish and lake trout.

Much further south, the lake fronts Detroit. Like the cities on Huron's northern islands, this industrial giant was founded as a small fur-trading post. Situated where it could tap the flow of raw materials between lakes Erie and Huron, Detroit grew to be America's fifth-largest city, with the help of Henry Ford's Model T. Now the city is changing: Challenged by a struggling auto industry and increasing water pollution, "Motor City" has diversified and reorganized. Today, only one city worker in ten is employed in the automotive field. The waterfront, an eyesore not long ago, now prides itself on its gleaming Renaissance Center, from whose expansive lobby one can actually look *south* into Canada.

*L*ocated *just east of the Straits of Mackinac, Mackinac Island (below)*

offers views of lakes Huron and Michigan.

*T*he Grand Hotel on Mackinac Island sits on a bluff high above Lake Huron. Built from the island's indigenous white pine, the structure has the world's longest porch, perhaps to accommodate the seemingly endless vistas.

*O*scada, Michigan's harbor was once filled with
logging ships.   Today, vacationers visit the area for its
scenic drives, boat trips, and fabulous trout fishing.

*S*portfishing in the Great Lakes is an angler's dream. Lake Huron's Georgian Bay is filled with delicious Coho salmon, and wildlife stalkers can spot white-tailed deer, red fox, mink, porcupine, and beaver on its wooded shores.

PART FOUR

Lake Michigan

Though it is the only Great Lake that lies completely within the United States, Lake Michigan hosts a surprising smorgasbord of foreign festivities. In the mid-nineteenth century, unprecedented numbers of Northern Europeans emigrated to America and settled in the pastoral hills of Michigan and Wisconsin surrounding Lake Michigan. Accustomed to hard labor, they cleared forests, tilled farms, erected mills, and connected streams with canals to build a network for floating traffic that moved to and from the Great Lake. The founders of the many new towns in the area maintained a fierce pride in their European heritage.

Today, the old-world customs are still alive on the lake's shores. The citizens of Holland, Michigan celebrate their Dutch ancestry by hosting a yearly tulip festival. Milwaukee's German roots are evident not only in the city's numerous breweries, but in its hearty food as well. Wisconsin produces the greatest variety of bratwurst and sausage in North America in addition to its famous dairy products, and wurst cookoffs are

The view from Door County's Potawatomi Park (previous page) has delighted visitors for years. While the harbor may be spotted with boats, the land still looks much as it did to eighteenth-century explorers. A vintage, hand-cranked ferry runs across the Kalamazoo River between the Michigan towns of Douglas and Saugatuck (previous page inset). This boat has traveled the same course for over one hundred years.

conducted with gusto at annual Oktoberfests throughout the state. The seventy-mile Door Peninsula in Wisconsin attracts throngs of visitors to its Norwegian festivals.

Northern Wisconsin and Michigan are covered with thick pine and deciduous forests and orchards. In May, the hills near Traverse City, Michigan, are white with cherry blossoms. In autumn, the landscape is ablaze with the brilliant fall foliage. Just west of the area, Sleeping Bear Dune–a veritable mountain of sand–rises four hundred feet above Lake Michigan. The six hundred-acre expanse became Sleeping Bear Dune National Lakeshore, a federally protected national park, in 1970.

While the lakefront is home to such ancient wonders, other areas of its shoreline are thoroughly contemporary. Positioned at the southern tip of Lake Michigan, Chicago links America's wheat fields and cattle farms to the industrial ports of the East Coast. Accordingly, millions of tons of grain, meat, steel, and other commodities from the Midwest passed through Chicago each year.

When Montgomery Ward built his mail-order company's

During its Tulip Time celebration, Holland's Veldheer Gardens are carpeted with over two million blossoms. Eight million more line the village's European-style streets and canals.

offices near there in the 1880s, Chicago's lakeshore was a wasteland of dumping grounds and railroad yards. Disgusted by the sight, Ward battled almost single-handedly to clean up the area. One hundred years later, that waterfront is a tribute to Ward's efforts. Chicagoans can spend their lunch hours swimming at Oak Street Beach or picnicking in Lincoln Park beneath the city's legendary skyscrapers. On weekends, the marinas are alive with activity, as sailors cast off to enjoy Lake Michigan's waters.

*S*ix Flags Over America (left) is a sprawling theme park in Gurnee, Illinois. One of the park's most popular rides is the American Eagle, a double-racing wooden roller coaster. Chicago's Wrigley Field (above), home of the Chicago Cubs, is a grand, old-style ballpark, complete with ivy-covered walls. After a heated debate, lights were finally added for night games in August, 1988.

Wisconsin's Sturgeon Bay (right) is an ideal recreation spot, because its waters are warmer than those in adjoining Green Bay. The area's surrounding wetlands offer refuge for various birds and mammals. Douglas, Michigan (below) lies inland from Lake Michigan on the Kalamazoo river. Passengers can cruise the area in an authentic sternwheel paddleboat or more modern craft, like those at this yacht club.

*N*orwegian immigrants founded Ephraim, Wisconsin in the mid-nineteenth century. The town's original dock and waterfront buildings still stand, though they feature twentieth-century embellishment.

*T*he area outside Traverse City, Michigan yields seventy-eight million

pounds of cherries every year. The annual July Cherry Festival features parades,

a queen's coronation, and, of course, pie-eating contests.

*E*phraim, Wisconsin's Scandinavian settlers and lumberjacks invented the "fish boil," a delicious way to prepare whitefish. The ritual combines fish, potatoes, plenty of onions, and more in a huge, steaming pot.

*T*he sand dunes along Lake Michigan's southern coast (below) have captivated men for centuries. Indiana Dunes State Park offers miles of waterfront for those who want to wander far from the crowds.

*S*leeping Bear Dune (right), in northern Michigan, comprises thirty-four square miles of fine white sand. Hikers climb the dune by foot to marvel at its overwhelming size.

Milwaukee's annual Summerfest (right) is billed as the "World's Greatest Music Festival," with concerts, parades, circuses, and impromptu entertainment. This melodious ensemble demonstrates a less strenuous alternative to the marching band. Milwaukee (below) is more a collection of small, traditional towns than one great city. The metropolis' diverse European heritage, dominated by Germans, is celebrated with its yearly Ethnic Parade.

*E*phraim's *Fyr Bal* festival commemorates the ancient Norse tradition of
Mid-Summer Eve. Feasting, dancing, and blazing fires welcome the second half
of the summer.

*S*augatuck, Michigan features dozens of quaint wooden buildings like Peterson Mills (below). Plentiful willows weep around it as if posing for a picture. In the artist community of Saugatuck (right), no space is too pedestrian for a creative paintbrush. This restroom adds new life to an average Sunday in the park.

Lake Superior

*T*he Split Rock Lighthouse *(previous page) served as sentinel from its perch high above Lake Superior from 1910 to 1968. It is still the tallest lighthouse in the United States. Historic Fort William (previous page inset), in Canada's Thunder Bay, is a hand-hewn reconstruction of the North West Company's main post, built in 1816. The original fort was built here in 1678. Copper Harbor on the Keweenaw Peninsula (left) is the northernmost point in Michigan. During the winter, the region may be covered with twenty feet of snow. Superior's shoreline is marked by rocky cliffs and wind-twisted trees (top left). The landscape has remained largely unchanged for the last two hundred years.*

Any description of Lake Superior is bound to be filled with superlatives. The largest and cleanest of the Great Lakes, Superior also has the deepest waters, the most rugged shoreline, the coldest winters, and the most recorded shipwrecks. It holds an astonishing ten percent of the earth's fresh water, and it has the greatest surface area of any lake in the world. Its cities claim records, too. Located twenty-three hundred miles from the Atlantic Ocean at the head of the Great Lakes/St. Lawrence waterway, Duluth, Minnesota is America's greatest inland seaport in terms of shipping tonnage. Further up the shore, Thunder Bay holds the largest grain elevators in the world and is the center of Canada's largest pulp- and paper-producing area. As a result, the Soo Locks at Superior's eastern end are among the world's busiest.

Though this inland sea is relatively untamed, most residents consider it a gentle giant. Visitors are amazed by the rocky beauty of the surrounding wilderness, much of which hasn't changed since white men first set foot there. The landscape is broken by craggy hills and stands of pine, balsam, birch, and aspen. Hikers walk all day on ancient Indian trails, interrupted only by the call of a distant loon. Fishermen pull brook trout from the meandering streams or dip-net tubs full of smelt from the many rivers that flow from Superior. The lake itself offers walleyes, bass, lake trout, and more.

Isle Royale, Superior's largest island, is nine miles wide, forty-five miles long, and ninety-nine percent wilderness. In the last several years, the island has been used to study the predator-prey relationship between wolves and moose. To preserve the area's unique ecosystem, no motorized vehicles are allowed on it. Thus, Isle Royale acts as an isolated wilderness laboratory, allowing naturalists a unique opportunity to observe the wolf and moose populations in their habitat.

Wisconsin's Apostle Islands lie off the American shore and are somewhat more settled than Isle Royale. Pleasure boats skim their sparkling waters, while landlubbers fish or hike on shore. Swimming, when possible, is particularly exhilarating because of the water's cold temperature. Ferries operate regularly between the islands for most of

*T*hunder Bay, at the western edge of the Great Lakes/St. Lawrence waterway, is big enough to accommodate any ship on the lake. Pleasure boats too small to venture out onto Superior cruise the bay easily as well.

Lake Superior's waters funnel into the St. Mary's River at Sault Ste. Marie, Michigan (left). The Soo Locks there operate throughout the icy winter. The Duluth, Mesabi, and Iron Range Railroad meets Lake Superior at Two Harbors, Minnesota (right). Millions of tons of iron ore and other commodities pass through this depot each year.

the year, but during the winter months residents actually drive their cars over frozen parts of the lake to the mainland and back.

Sailors who venture north beyond Thunder Bay may witness miraculous celestial events. When the conditions are right, the night sky becomes a magnificent planetarium with spectacular displays of Aurora Borealis (the Northern Lights) and meteor showers. Such natural wonders are fitting for a lake of Superior's magnitude.

*I*sle Royale (top left) was designated a National Park in 1931, "to conserve a prime example of Northwoods Wilderness." Naturalists there study the relationship between the island's moose and wolves. Michigan's Pictured Rocks National Lakeshore (left) includes spectacular glacier-carved rock. The State government has recently made moves to preserve the spot. The Gooseberry River (above) cuts through the rugged forests of logging country and splits into five separate waterfalls before tumbling into Lake Superior.

69

*M*ichigan's Keweenaw Peninsula (left) reaches sixty miles into Lake Superior. The region's quiet inland lakes are perfect for a relaxing day of canoeing. The success of Minnesota's ore industry brought the famous whaleback ships (above) to Lake Superior. Their distinctive design allowed them to carry heavy cargo and still ride high on the water.

*T*wo Harbors, Minnesota (above) became a vital shipping terminal in the late nineteenth century. Ships carried cargoes of minerals east from the twin harbors of Agate and Burlington Bays. Ewen, in Michigan's Upper Peninsula, is home to the "Load of Logs" (left). These fifty pine logs were dragged over ice and snow to the 1893 Chicago World's Fair and back. They have rested here ever since.